WHA̓

Kurt Jenkins has a passion for God and for the developing and releasing of leaders. This book will help any leader to meditate upon and apply the principles of leadership embedded in the Proverbs. For thousands of years, these Proverbs have been a source of wisdom in leading people, leading yourself, and navigating complicated issues within organizations and in life.

—Jeff Leake
Lead Pastor, Allison Park Church
President, Reach Northeast Network

Everyday Leadership does an amazing job getting to the heart of the matter—the heart. Kurt has approached leadership development in a fresh and relevant way that will take the reader to the next level.

—Ron Showers
Senior Director of Community Development
Convoy of Hope

Short, sweet, and to the right point! This book will help you and your team to grow together with the thirty-one-day leadership challenge.

—Tom Rees
Director of Church Planting and Development
Penn-Del Ministry Network

EVERYDAY LEADERSHIP

THE GUIDING PRINCIPLES OF PROVERBS

EVERYDAY LEADERSHIP

KURT JENKINS

TATE PUBLISHING
AND ENTERPRISES, LLC

Everyday Leadership
Copyright © 2015 by Kurt Jenkins. All rights reserved.

No part of this publication may be reproduced, stored in a retrieval system or transmitted in any way by any means, electronic, mechanical, photocopy, recording or otherwise without the prior permission of the author except as provided by USA copyright law.

All scripture quotations, unless otherwise indicated, are taken from the *Holy Bible, New International Version*®, NIV®. Copyright ©1973, 1978, 1984, 2011 by Biblica, Inc.™ Used by permission of Zondervan. All rights reserved worldwide. www.zondervan.com

Scripture quotations marked (NIV) are taken from the *Holy Bible, New International Version*®, NIV®. Copyright © 1973, 1978, 1984, 2011 by Biblica, Inc.™ Used by permission of Zondervan. All rights reserved worldwide. www.zondervan.com

Scripture quotations marked (NLT) are taken from the *Holy Bible, New Living Translation*, copyright © 1996. Used by permission of Tyndale House Publishers, Inc., Wheaton, Illinois 60189. All rights reserved.

This book is designed to provide accurate and authoritative information with regard to the subject matter covered. This information is given with the understanding that neither the author nor Tate Publishing, LLC is engaged in rendering legal, professional advice. Since the details of your situation are fact dependent, you should additionally seek the services of a competent professional.

The opinions expressed by the author are not necessarily those of Tate Publishing, LLC.

Published by Tate Publishing & Enterprises, LLC
127 E. Trade Center Terrace | Mustang, Oklahoma 73064 USA
1.888.361.9473 | www.tatepublishing.com

Tate Publishing is committed to excellence in the publishing industry. The company reflects the philosophy established by the founders, based on Psalm 68:11,

"The Lord gave the word and great was the company of those who published it."

Book design copyright © 2015 by Tate Publishing, LLC. All rights reserved.
Cover design by Brian Mezerski and Nino Carlo Suico
Interior design by Manolito Bastasa

Published in the United States of America

ISBN: 978-1-62024-669-6
1. Religion / Christian Life / Devotional
2. Religion / Leadership
15.05.29

I dedicate this book to my heavenly Father and my earthly father, for whom writing was a natural gift. What each penned is eternal.

INTRODUCTION

Everyday Leadership is a compilation of three month-long devotionals to help advance your spiritual growth in the area of Christian leadership. Whether you are learning how to lead, your leadership has hit a plateau, or you are a thriving leader, this book will help you lead every day.

A question many Christians ask themselves is, "How do I know if I am a leader?" The answer is simple. If you can answer yes to any of the following questions, then you are a leader because you have the potential to positively influence the lives of others.

- Do your beliefs and faith impact anyone else other than yourself?
- Do your behaviors and attitudes affect those around you?
- Are there other people who ask you for advice and counsel?
- Are you responsible for giving instructions or guidance to others?
- Is there at least one person who has followed your example in life?

We have complicated the definition of leadership. Leadership happens whenever you have people following you in any circumstance or situation in life. It doesn't have to happen in a boardroom or executive meeting. Your children, neighbors, coworkers, and church family represent just a few spheres of influence you have in which people are following you. Whether you know it or not, whether you like it or not, you are perceived as a leader in these spheres.

Being aware of this will drastically affect the amount of positive influence you have in the lives of others. Understanding what people are expecting from you will also help you lead them toward their goals and, ultimately, toward Christ. Your leadership requires constant growth so you can help keep those following you on God's path in their lives.

THE PLAN

- Read **one** chapter of Proverbs each day of the month.
- Listen for **one** minute to what the Holy Spirit is saying to you.
- Take **one** minute to read a brief leadership principle from that day's Proverb.
- Write at least **one** way you can implement that principle into your life.

THE FLOW

Each day has four sections:

- **Verse**—Verse(s) of the day taken from the book of Proverbs.
- **Thought**—A brief leadership principle based on that verse.
- **Challenge**—Thoughts and questions to help connect the principle to your daily life.
- **Action**—The action you are going to take to implement the principle that day.

WHAT *EVERYDAY LEADERSHIP* IS NOT

- **It is not something to be taken lightly.**

    Dedicate yourself to aggressive growth. In our culture, it can be easy to take the responsibility of leading for granted. We have our smart phones, social networks, video conferencing, and many other easy-to-use tools for leading and connecting with others. However, the more tools we use, the easier it becomes to fake it and not let leadership penetrate our hearts. Be extremely intentional to allow the Lord to stretch you, and take you to new levels of leadership than ever before.

- **It is not a checklist to complete.**

  Take time to listen to the Lord's voice. Life is busy enough as it is, with too many people telling us their thoughts and opinions. We can get caught up in the rush of the day and end up checking off our to-do list just to find ourselves moving along to the next day. True leadership will develop by stopping and taking time to actually listen to what God is saying to you through His Word. That doesn't mean simply stopping to read my comments or other study notes. Listening to the Lord's voice means reading the daily Proverb and then stopping to listen, in complete silence, to what He is saying to you.

- **It is not a theological study of Proverbs.**

  These are brief thoughts, not a doctrinal commentary. They were birthed out of my personal time with God, where I feel He gave me revelation on small portions of each Proverb. Look at it as my own journey of learning that I have invited you to take with me.

- **It is not a one-way leadership training.**

  Communicating your thoughts helps activate new attitudes and behaviors. If you're like me, you've read several books in the past with great principles that apply to your life. By the time you are done reading, you have not applied a single principle. This book is different. It is a two-way leadership journey. Each day ends with a challenge that begs to be answered. This is your chance to put in writing what God is leading you to do, or a lesson from the Proverbs that He has highlighted to you. Don't overanalyze your thoughts. Just begin writing in faith that God has already spoken to you and that you are writing His ideas on the paper. And have fun doing it!

MONTH 1

DAY 1: PROVERBS 1

VERSE

The fear of the LORD is the beginning of knowledge.
(Proverbs 1:7)

THOUGHT

In today's culture, successful leadership is often defined
by self-effort, accomplishments, and status. In society, the
foundation of knowledge comes from the best books, training videos, and conference speakers. For Christians, successful leadership is defined by our interaction with God.
We must always build our foundation on the fear of the
Lord. This fear is a reverence that drives us toward him, not
a fear of punishment that pushes us away. Fear of the Lord
is a believer's natural response to how awesome He is. It is
the feeling you get when you become aware of how holy
and tremendous God is, while fully appreciating that He
still allows us to be near Him.

CHALLENGE

If you are trying to develop yourself as a leader using only the methods of society, stop! Take time today to worship in reverence and awe of our God, and let Him lay the foundation of true wisdom and knowledge by simply being in His presence. How will you worship the Lord differently today than you have in the past? What is God saying to you about developing your level of true biblical fear of the Lord? What are you going to do about it?

ACTION

looking at names of God
- how / when / situations as
God reveals Himself
- sequentially in relationship
to people - Jesus -
Abraham, Isaac, Jacob

DAY 2: PROVERBS 2

VERSE

Cry out for insight, and ask for understanding. Search for them as you would silver; seek them like hidden treasures. (Proverbs 2:3–4, NLT)

THOUGHT

Leaders take initiative. They don't wait for things to happen; they cause things to happen. They are trailblazers who set the course of action for those around them. Leaders know how to respond to situations rather than reacting to problems. Crying out for insight and understanding builds our faith that God will bring breakthroughs in all areas of our lives. When you face a problem, cry out for the solution. When conflict comes your way, search for understanding as you would silver. When your followers stop growing, seek creative ways to ignite them as you would seek a hidden treasure. Take as much initiative to search for insight and understanding as you did the last time you lost your car keys when you were running late for an appointment.

CHALLENGE

As a leader, don't wait around and expect a breakthrough to magically appear. Cry out today for more insight, more understanding, and more of the Lord. What specific breakthrough do you need right now that requires divine insight? Write down one way you are going to cry out for it starting today. For example, you can read through several Psalms until you find clarity for your circumstances. Or you can begin a fast today until God brings the needed breakthrough. Listen for the voice of the Lord, then begin to take action.

ACTION

Being able to bring a word
of Life to the kids at
Wash. Estates

— they have no sense (generally)
of who they are —

Created in God's image
+ His unique design.
Ps 139:13 ff

DAY 3: PROVERBS 3

VERSE

Let love and faithfulness never leave you…. Then you will win favor and a good name in the sight of God and man. (Proverbs 3:3–4)

[handwritten note: no— Leaving / Lakeview / Lost Rel'n]

THOUGHT

As leaders, we often have to make difficult decisions that will upset other people. The decision itself isn't what damages our long-term relationships; it is the attitude in which we make our decisions. Leaders need to demonstrate love and faithfulness during these delicate times. Our followers need to know that we value our relationship with them over our need to be right and that our loyalty to them outweighs our need to have our own way. Godly leaders can make the hard decisions the Lord is calling them to make without running over everyone in their path. This results in having favor with both God and people.

CHALLENGE

Who have you offended or hurt recently because you had the wrong attitude during a hard decision you had to make? How and when will you admit you were wrong and seek to restore love and faithfulness to that relationship? If you can't think of a specific situation, write some thoughts about how you can go and make it right with another person in the event that it does occur in the future.

ACTION

personal contact - not text - need body language + tones of voice -

With Aaron - avoid snippiness and letting my anger three -

DAY 4: PROVERBS 4

VERSE

Guard your heart above all else, for it determines the course of your life. Look straight ahead, and fix your eyes on what lies before you. Mark out a straight path for your feet; stay on the safe path. Don't get sidetracked; keep your feet from following evil. (Proverbs 4:23, 25–27, NLT)

problem —
I have
no vision

THOUGHT

Every good leader has a vision for their life. Proverbs 4 gives very clear instruction on how to make sure this vision (course of your life) is accomplished. Be diligent about guarding your heart from sin, unforgiveness, bitterness, perverse talk, evil, and anything else that would take your focus off of the path God has set before you. Marking a straight path for your feet requires you to make certain decisions before the temptations arise. You can already say no to a flirtatious coworker before he/she crosses your path. You can already decide not to make dishonest financial transactions before you find yourself in that situation. Taking risks and making mistakes doesn't sidetrack leaders from their vision; an unguarded heart does.

CHALLENGE

In a few sentences, write out a brief vision you feel God has for your life. What are some areas in which your heart is currently unguarded that will negatively affect this vision? How will you go about guarding it and marking a straight path for your feet?

ACTION

I have none - never had
defined goals -
Now - interest in some form
of personal helping (mentoring
- signed up for
Light University course
1/25/2022
At Lakeview - I had a prophetic
roll - but not yet
at Central -

DAY 5: PROVERBS 5

VERSE

I would not obey my teachers or listen to my instructors. And I was soon in serious trouble in the assembly of God's people. (Proverbs 5:13–14)

THOUGHT

This verse deals with adultery, which I trust is on your radar to avoid at all cost. However, it is profound what comments are made by the one who has fallen into sexual sin. "I would not obey my teachers…instructors." Godly leaders surround themselves with godly counsel—friends, accountability partners, and mentors who can speak honestly to them in order to correct, and even rebuke, if needed. If you don't have these people in place now while you are doing fine, you will not permit them to speak into your life if you are ever deceived or trapped in sin.

CHALLENGE

Write the names of two to four people who you can surround yourself with to make sure someone is in place to correct you if you fall into sexual (or other) sin. When will you contact them to discuss this? How will you go about sharing your ideas? Remember, this is going to position you to end your race well.

ACTION

_____

_____

_____

_____

_____

DAY 6: PROVERBS 6

VERSE

A little sleep, a little slumber, a little folding of the hands to rest—and poverty will come on you like a thief. (Proverbs 6:10–11)

THOUGHT

Leadership in society is marked by working long hours, being away from family, and exhausting yourself to get more done. I don't think this is what verse 10 is talking about. Leaders need rest. We work best when we are fresh and energized. These verses aren't addressing sleep as much as they are addressing procrastination. We often find that time lines, deadlines, and goals are not met due to procrastination. A wise leader will steward their time effectively by working when it's time to work so they can rest when it's time to rest. For example, a few verses before verse 10, it talks about the wisdom of ants, which work and store up provisions in summer for the winter. These ants, as tiny as they are, use a huge amount of wisdom in stewarding their time and energy well.

CHALLENGE

List one project in any area of your life that you have been putting off doing. Now set a deadline and write the date below. Summarize the next step you can take today to end your procrastination.

ACTION

_____

_____

_____

_____

_____

DAY 7: PROVERBS 7

VERSE

With persuasive words she led him astray; she seduced him with her smooth talk. (Proverbs 7:21)

THOUGHT

Whether it's an adulterer, a manipulator, or a self-serving person, leaders will inevitably interact with others who try to force their own plans. Sure, they will talk about the beautiful sights, the wonderful smells, and the exciting experiences that they have in store for us. Unfortunately, it never seems to work out that way. We must be confident in what God is calling us to accomplish and aggressive in resisting the temptation to leave that path for the path of others, however enticing it may look.

CHALLENGE

Identify several people in your spheres of influence who may be trying to derail you from the purposes God has for your life. How will you talk with them privately, in grace and love, to communicate the direction you are taking and why? In what ways will you ask them to support you and partner with you in these endeavors?

ACTION

_____

_____

_____

_____

_____

DAY 8: PROVERBS 8

VERSE

At the highest point along the way, where the paths meet, she takes her stand; beside the gates leading into the city, at the entrances, she cries aloud. (Proverbs 8:2–3)

THOUGHT

The Lord positions leaders to have wisdom and understanding at key moments in life. It is during these times that our ministries, businesses, families, etc., can find great favor and blessing.

- on the heights—This refers to mountaintop experiences in life when we can become complacent or too relaxed because we have a good view of life and things seem to be going well.
- where the paths meet—NLT calls this a crossroads, where important decisions that will affect the direction you travel for the next season of life need to be made.

- beside the gates—This is a place of defense against enemies. When we are being attacked and accused, we must use wisdom in how we respond while allowing the Lord to be our defense.
- at the entrances—This is the place of new opportunities. Good stewardship of new opportunities will position us for a greater breakthrough in the future.

CHALLENGE

We need wisdom and understanding in all areas of life, and we need to discern when the Lord is calling out for us to listen. What is the Lord saying to you in this season of life? What changes need to occur in this season that will prepare you for the next?

ACTION

_____

_____

_____

_____

_____

DAY 9: PROVERBS 9

VERSE

Do not rebuke mockers or they will hate you; rebuke the wise man and they will love you. (Proverbs 9:8)

THOUGHT

Good leaders choose wisely in whom they invest their time and resources. Unfortunately, every leader has mockers. Mockers are those who treat others with contempt, either out in the open or privately through gossip and complaining. Yes, even in the church, all leaders have mockers. Mockers don't take a rebuke well, but a wise man or woman will. Who you are going to invest yourself in is a critical decision you must make. You still have to lead mockers, but it is unwise to invest much time and resource into them since their motives are against you. Find others who are learners, who trust you, who want to grow with you, who see your vision, and pour your life into them. They will love you for it, even when you have to rebuke them.

CHALLENGE

Who is one person you can begin investing in, and what is one way you can do it today? Who is one person who is draining you through complaints and mockery, and how can you begin to distance yourself from them?

ACTION

_____

_____

_____

_____

_____

DAY 10: PROVERBS 10

VERSE

Too much talk leads to sin. Be sensible and keep
your mouth shut. (Proverbs 10:19, NLT)

THOUGHT

Honor is a core value of leadership. When you talk about
another person to someone else, you are either honoring
them or dishonoring them with your words. There are no
neutral words; they are either building up or tearing down.
Even when we disagree with the beliefs, opinions, and
behaviors of another, we can still honor them for who they
are and not stumble over who they *aren't*. At times, we just
need to keep quiet if we can't find an honorable word to
say. When we find ourselves in conversations where others
are gossiping, complaining, or accusing, we can't wait until
that moment to decide whether to join in on the conversation or not. If we already have honor as a core value, we will
"keep our mouth shut" and take a stand by what we don't
say, rather than by what we do say.

CHALLENGE

Take a moment right now to reflect on the conversations you have had in the past two days. Did your words honor or dishonor others? How can you become more honoring with your words?

ACTION

_____

_____

_____

_____

_____

DAY 11: PROVERBS 11

VERSE

Through the blessing of the upright a city is exalted.
(Proverbs 11:11)

THOUGHT

Christian leaders can ask for many years for revival to come upon our cities and see no results if we ourselves are not being a blessing to our cities. Yes, revival will come from God, but it will flow through his people. Once we take personal responsibility for the holistic discipleship of our entire city (community, school district, etc.), our city will be exalted. The NLT says, "Upright citizens are good for a city and make it prosper." We are supposed to be conduits of God's blessing, prosperity, and favor to a group of people who have yet to meet Him. How awesome would that be for Christian leaders to change the entire atmosphere of a city to a point where crime decreases, employment increases, families are restored, and more churches need to be opened! Leaders can live in such a way to initiate revival instead of waiting for one to arrive.

CHALLENGE

Pray today for God to give you insight on how you can bless your city/community by being an upright citizen. What is one action you will take today to be that blessing?

ACTION

_____

_____

_____

_____

_____

DAY 12: PROVERBS 12

VERSE

Truthful lips endure forever, but a lying tongue lasts only a moment. (Proverbs 12:19)

THOUGHT

This seems almost too elementary to be a leadership principle, but telling the truth is still really, really important. The Bible says it can even determine how long you endure as one with influence in the lives of others. To get us all on the same page, let's break it down.

- small lie—Lying
- little white lie—Lying
- exaggeration—Lying
- withholding information—Lying
- rounding up or rounding down when it counts—Lying
- telling someone "it's no big deal" when they have offended you—Lying
- telling the truth—Not Lying

I want my words to "endure forever" and to be an encouragement for the generations to come, but I still find myself lying at times. How about you?

CHALLENGE

In what situations or areas of life do you lie the most? Examine your conversations over the next twenty-four hours and evaluate how truthful you are. What do you need to change in regards to telling the truth?

ACTION

_____

_____

_____

_____

_____

DAY 13: PROVERBS 13

VERSE

Hope deferred makes the heart sick, but a longing
[dream] fulfilled is a tree of life. A longing [dream]
fulfilled is sweet to the soul, but fools detest turning
from evil. (Proverbs 13:12, 19)

THOUGHT

As leaders, it's time to dream again. I will not settle for
the excuses of some adults saying, "Only kids can dream
big because they haven't experienced the reality of life yet."
People who say that are simply afraid to think big themselves, so they don't want anyone else to either. The reason
kids can dream so big is because they haven't met enough
"experienced" adults who have rationalized their big ideas
to the point of neutralizing them. It is not childish at all
to believe that God wants to do amazing and significant
things in our life.

If Abraham was able to look into a crystal-clear sky and
dream of his descendants being more numerous than the
stars, we can still dream today. If Noah was able to envi-

sion a boat large enough to fit two of every kind of animal, then we can envision God doing huge things through us. If Mary was able to believe that she was carrying someone eternal, then we can believe the same.

CHALLENGE

I don't remember one time in the Bible where God asked someone to rationalize the assignment before he sent them off to do something great. Will you dare to dream again? What dream has God placed in your heart that has either died or is lying dormant for fear of rejection or ridicule? How can you allow God to bring this dream back to life?

ACTION

_____

_____

_____

_____

_____

DAY 14: PROVERBS 14

VERSE

Where there are no oxen, the manger is empty, but from the strength of an ox comes abundant harvests. (Proverbs 14:4)

THOUGHT

The NLT says that "without oxen a stable stays clean." That's nice for the one who cleans the manger, but not for the farmer, his family, the other animals, and the community, who all depend on the farmer's harvest to survive. The farmer is working for an abundant harvest. He needs lots of strong oxen to bring in this size of harvest. Lots of oxen mean lots of messes in the stable.

If we, as leaders, truly want an abundant harvest, then we have to be willing to deal with and clean up lots of messes. If you are interested in a nice, neat, clean life and ministry, you won't make an impact on many people, but your manger will be spotless. If you desire to see a true harvest, you have to be willing to work with addicts, the homeless, and those who are not easily accepted by others. Your manger will need cleaning quite often, but you will also be the one who reaps the reward of a bountiful harvest.

CHALLENGE

It's your choice. What are you going to do? In what areas of your life are you being too safe, simply trying to keep them clean? How can you step out of your comfort zone in the next twenty-four hours and put yourself in a situation that may lead to a mess? Just remember, that mess may also lead to an abundant harvest!

ACTION

_____

_____

_____

_____

_____

DAY 15: PROVERBS 15

VERSE

A cheerful look brings joy to the heart, and good news gives health to the bones. (Proverbs 15:30)

THOUGHT

Leadership guru John Maxwell, in his book *25 Ways to Win with People*, explains how he practices what he calls the thirty-second rule, where he gives attention, affirmation, and appreciation within the first thirty seconds of a conversation. This principle aligns nicely with the Bible, where it says that a smile and an encouraging word can have profound effects on another person's heart and health. The devil has enough people working to discourage and demean those with whom you interact. We have the opportunity during every conversation to counter that with a cheerful look and some good news. Trying this principle and biblical truth may very well make someone's day and provide the boost they need to bring them back to health in various areas of their life.

CHALLENGE

What are some ways you can begin showing your appreciation of others in conversation? In what setting will you first be most intentional about applying this?

ACTION

_____

_____

_____

_____

_____

DAY 16: PROVERBS 16

VERSE

In their hearts humans plans their course, but the
LORD determines their steps. (Proverbs 16:9)

THOUGHT

Every Christian leader faces the balancing act of wise
planning and being Spirit-led. There is much fruit in sitting down, listening to the voice of the Lord, and creating
short- and long-term plans for ministry, business, family,
and life. These plans provide a framework to operate within
on a daily basis and set our expectations high for what God
can accomplish. However, we must be willing to deviate
from those plans at any moment the Holy Spirit prompts.
We should learn to live by God's presence and not just
our principles. Principles set the boundaries, but His presence is what actually navigates us through the specifics of
daily living.

CHALLENGE

Yes, write out the plans you feel the Lord is giving you; *yes*, write out goals for different areas of your life; and *yes*, be sensitive to the leading of the Holy Spirit at all times. It is not an either-or but a both-and. What do you tend to lean more toward? Writing out your plans or spontaneously following the Holy Spirit? How are you going to balance the two?

ACTION

_____

_____

_____

_____

_____

DAY 17: PROVERBS 17

VERSE

Whoever would foster love covers over an offense, but whoever repeats the matter separates close friends. (Proverbs 17:9)

THOUGHT

When Jesus defended the adulterous woman from her accusers, He *did not* tell everyone all her sins so that she would feel the pain of her sin before she was forgiven. He *did not* take her back to his pastoral office and rebuke her so that she would be fully aware of what she had done. He didn't even say, "You know, you have hurt a lot of people in the past few years." No, he covered her offense to the point that no one else was even able to condemn her or pass judgment. She was freed by grace.

This is what leaders do. Instead of making sure the person feels the pain of their sin, a leader will quickly pick up the one who has fallen and restore them in love. A leader will cover the sin, not to be secretive or to put others at risk, but to ensure that the person will feel powerful and free afterward. When we make the person feel small, or when we share their sins with other people, they are not truly being restored. They are actually being demeaned to a place that falls short of God's grace.

CHALLENGE

He who has been forgiven much loves much. The Bible doesn't say anything about condemning them or making them feel bad first. If you have shared someone's sins with another, go and ask for forgiveness from the person who has sinned and from the one with whom you shared it. What adjustments need to occur in your daily life so that you can begin living with Jesus's way of dealing with sin?

ACTION

_____

_____

_____

_____

_____

DAY 18: PROVERBS 18

VERSE

A gift opens the way for the giver and ushers the giver into the presence of the great. (Proverbs 18:16)

THOUGHT

Leadership is all about giving gifts: gifts of knowledge, gifts of wisdom, gifts of resources, gifts of love, gifts of time, gifts of counsel, gifts of energy, gifts of emotion, gifts of teaching, gifts of forgiveness, gifts of inspiration, gifts of encouragement, gifts of correction, gifts of advice, gifts of prayer, and much more.

I used to get frustrated when small-group leaders didn't come to the meetings or when the ushers didn't show up on time. Then I realized that I was expecting them to give to me instead of focusing on what I could give to them, like clear communication and good training. We don't lead to receive. We lead to give to others, to equip them for greater service, to mobilize them in their strengths, to release them into their God-given destiny.

Proverbs also says that giving gifts results in you having an audience with influential people. We should desire to have influence in the lives of principals, mayors, judges, and CEOs so our impact on them will be multiplied by the people in whom they influence.

CHALLENGE

Write down three ways in which you can give to those who follow you the next time you gather.

ACTION

_____

_____

_____

_____

_____

DAY 19: PROVERBS 19

VERSE

A hot-tempered person must pay the penalty; rescue them, and you will have to do it again. (Proverbs 19:19)

THOUGHT

One of the best lessons anyone can learn in life is that actions have consequences, both good and bad. Leaders can best serve their teams by helping them make good choices that affect their actions so they will experience positive consequences. However, tempers will still flare, mistakes will still be made, and negative consequences will still be experienced. The key during negative consequences is to empower people and not enable them. Enabling is the continuous rescuing of someone who deliberately makes wrong choices, which, in turn, prohibits the person from experiencing the negative consequence. A leader may think they are truly rescuing the person, but they are really keeping the person from learning a valuable lesson that will empower them for future decisions.

Empowering someone allows them to make both good and bad decisions with guidance on how to take personal responsibility for the consequences they face. Either way, the person comes out of the situation stronger and wiser because they were allowed to take ownership of their own problems. This way, the victory becomes theirs when the problem is solved.

CHALLENGE

Are you enabling or empowering people? Summarize a specific situation where you enabled and how you could have dealt with it differently? What do you need to change to be more empowering?

ACTION

_____

_____

_____

_____

_____

DAY 20: PROVERBS 20

VERSE

The purposes of a person's heart are deep waters, but one who has insight draws them out. (Proverbs 20:5)

THOUGHT

The original intent of this verse probably leans toward drawing out the hidden wrong motives of a man's heart that he is unaware of without wise counsel. I think we have done a thorough job judging the hidden (evil) motives of others for centuries. Instead of assuming people are bent toward evil, we should believe that other Christians are bent toward righteousness. Leaders should begin seeing others for who they are in Christ—born-again, a new creation, created in God's image, forgiven, a saint, part of the royal priesthood, a renewed mind. We will then begin approaching our people with the intent of drawing out the hidden potential, the suppressed passions, and the concealed purposes that God has planted deep within their soul.

We have the awesome privilege of going fishing in the deep waters of people's hearts to help reveal the divine destiny God has given them. We get to believe in them and highlight their skills and strengths while prophetically calling forth the very things God has purposed in their hearts, but they don't yet know exist within them.

CHALLENGE

The next time you talk with someone in your sphere of influence, be intentional about fishing for potential in their lives during your conversation. What one or two people come to mind right now in which you can do this? How will you purposefully create a conversation that will begin this process?

ACTION

_____

_____

_____

_____

_____

DAY 21: PROVERBS 21

VERSE

One who is wise can go up against the city of the mighty and pull down the stronghold in which they trust. (Proverbs 21:22)

THOUGHT

It seems unlikely that one man can overtake a mighty city and destroy the strength on which it relies. The man mentioned in this verse must have heard the saying "Work smarter, not harder." If you are in leadership and you would like to continue to lead for any length of time, you must learn to work smarter and not just harder. You can spend all your time working hard to look strong and invincible, but you will quickly tire out and exhaust your energy on human effort alone. Leaders know where to allocate their energy, time, and efforts to have the greatest impact in their sphere of influence. Thus, they depend on the wisdom of God to determine what to get involved with, what to say no to, and how to approach their daily tasks. They usually have to do tasks only once, where the harder workers often have to redo their tasks because of mistakes and overlooked details.

CHALLENGE

What is one area of your life where you have been working harder and not smarter? What will you do to begin working smarter? What areas of work, play, or ministry do you need to say no to in order to continue working smarter?

ACTION

_____

_____

_____

_____

_____

DAY 22: PROVERBS 22

VERSE

The lazy person claims, "There's a lion out there! If I go outside, I might be killed!" (Proverbs 22:13, NLT)

THOUGHT

Simply put, leaders aren't lazy. To avoid becoming lazy, we can identify three traits that usually lead to this detrimental lifestyle:

1. Blaming others for your own circumstances
2. Making excuses for why it isn't worth moving forward
3. Fearing risk so you never accomplish anything significant in your life

I believe these traits create a lazy person who neglects taking personal responsibility over their own decisions and life.

If God has established you as a Christian leader:

1. Stop blaming others for your circumstances and start thinking of solutions to the problems you face
2. Stop making excuses about all the negative stuff that might happen and take a step forward
3. Stop allowing fear to dictate your destiny

Set your eyes on living a life of significance for God then watch Him do it through you!

CHALLENGE

In what areas of your life are you being lazy? What is one risk you can take that will confront your fears, eliminate excuses, and push you further into your destiny?

ACTION

_____

_____

_____

_____

_____

DAY 23: PROVERBS 23

VERSE

Do not join those who drink too much wine or gorge themselves on meat. (Proverbs 23:20)

THOUGHT

Leadership is about having self-control so you can help others whose lives are out of control by bringing them back into balance. When someone lacks self-control, it will manifest in different areas of their lives, some more severe than others. It may come out in having unruly children, a fragile marriage, or an ineffective ministry; for others, it can be drinking too much alcohol or gorging themselves with food.

I don't believe verse 20 deals with enjoying a large buffet every once in a while; it deals with lifestyles and patterns of behavior. When you interact with someone who consistently shows a lack of self-control with external behaviors, you should begin to minister to their soul, which is where detrimental thoughts and attitudes begin. Almost always, there will be something out of place internally, which leads to chaos externally.

CHALLENGE

Verse 20 tells us not to join them, but I think what it means is, "Don't do what they do." I encourage you to join them by spending time with these people to find out how you can lift them up and bring control back to their lives without letting their behavior affect yours. How is this already happening in your life? How will you be more intentional about it in the future?

ACTION

_____

_____

_____

_____

_____

DAY 24: PROVERBS 24

VERSE

A person who plans evil will get a reputation as a troublemaker. (Proverbs 24:8, NLT)

THOUGHT

Our plans (or thoughts and motives) will eventually lead to actions, which over time establish our reputation. As leaders, our reputation should be important to us, but not in a way that leads to the fear of man by trying to please others at any cost. Our desire to have a reputation that is above reproach should be used as a checks-and-balances system for our motives and plans.

If we notice that our plans include aspects of selfishness or manipulation, the realization of how this will affect our reputation should bring us into check. However, instead of worrying about whether you are planning evil all the time, another way to look at this verse would be the opposite. A person who plans *good* will get a reputation as a *peacemaker*.

CHALLENGE

Are your plans, thoughts, and motives genuinely good? Are the actions that follow these plans creating peace or trouble? How can you help someone else you care about deeply who seems to make more trouble than peace?

ACTION

_____

_____

_____

_____

_____

DAY 25: PROVERBS 25

VERSE

Don't demand an audience with the king or push for a place among the great. It's better to wait for an invitation to the head table than to be sent away in public disgrace. (Proverbs 25:6–7, NLT)

THOUGHT

Probably the best lesson I've learned so far in Christian leadership is to get out of the way and allow the Lord to establish you in current and future positions. Trying to earn a promotion, a better job, or recognition usually ends up in disaster. It is much more fruitful to do the very best you can with your current responsibilities and allow the Lord to promote you in his timing. If we truly trust Him and work unto the Lord, then we don't live by the free-market system that the rest of the country does.

We don't need to force open doors of opportunity before God opens them. We don't need to build our résumé to get noticed. God already notices us. We don't need to worry about what position or title we hold since God will accomplish what He wants to no matter what our business card says.

CHALLENGE

If you are getting anxious in your current position, please do not try to force the hand of someone else, but rather wait patiently for the hand of God to establish and promote you. What situations in your life can you take a step back from and let the Lord take control?

ACTION

_____

_____

_____

_____

_____

DAY 26: PROVERBS 26

VERSE

Without wood a fire goes out; without gossip a quarrel dies down. (Proverbs 26:20)

THOUGHT

Leaders are responsible for creating the environment in which their followers function. This requires you to make sure the right characteristics are being fostered and that the wrong ones are eliminated. A ministry or business that is thriving and healthy can be killed in a short period of time if gossip or other unhealthy behavior develops without being confronted. On the other hand, when leaders are proactive at creating and preserving a healthy environment, there are many fires that will never begin and, consequently, will never have to be put out.

CHALLENGE

How can you be more intentional at creating a healthy environment in the areas you influence? List the fires that need to be put out now? When are you going to do it, and how?

ACTION

_____

_____

_____

_____

_____

DAY 27: PROVERBS 27

VERSE

The crucible for silver and the furnace for gold, but people are tested by their praise. (Proverbs 27:21)

THOUGHT

God created people with a need for acknowledgement, affirmation, and encouragement. However, the very thing that fills our emotional tank can also destroy us as leaders. We need to be able to receive praise and honor while staying humble. I don't agree with false humility, whereby you can barely compliment someone without them arguing that it wasn't them, that they are a piece of trash, and that it was only God. Well, God chose to use them and flow through them. They are His children and His masterpiece.

God is honored when His children are honored. When someone praises you in public, it allows you to praise God in private for building you up through the encouragement of others. There is a healthy middle ground between pride and false humility where Christian leaders can thrive and prosper.

CHALLENGE

How do you receive praise from others? Does anything need to change in this area?

ACTION

_____

_____

_____

_____

_____

DAY 28: PROVERBS 28

VERSE

Income from charging high interest rates will end up in the pocket of someone who is kind to the poor. Whoever gives to the poor will lack nothing, but those who close their eyes to poverty will be cursed. (Proverbs 28:8, 27, NLT)

THOUGHT

There seems to be connection between someone who is compassionate to the poor and God's trust in them as wise stewards of His resources. Verse 8 seems to hint at a transfer of wealth from those who are using it for the purpose of worldly advancement to those who will use it for the purpose of kingdom advancement. Then in verse 27, it speaks of the provision that will be supplied for the person who is caring for the poor.

It is important that we see both aspects of this financial process. God isn't transferring money from the sinner to the saint so we can have nicer cars. He is transferring it to us so we can put a purpose to it. On the other hand, He does promise to supply our needs when we properly steward the first provision.

CHALLENGE

How do you specifically give to and care for the poor? How can you steward your finances more wisely to give more effectively?

ACTION

_____

_____

_____

_____

_____

DAY 29: PROVERBS 29

VERSE

Fear of man will prove to be a snare, but whoever trusts in the LORD is kept safe. (Proverbs 29:25)

THOUGHT

Many leaders struggle with the fear of man while making decisions and determining direction in their organization, ministry, etc. The thoughts and opinions of others crowd out the voice of the Lord. While trying to stay safe, leaders will do things that they think will make people happy. In the end, they will realize that they can never please everyone.

It seems dangerous and risky to trust God's voice when it goes against the popular opinion of other believers, but it turns out to be the safest place you can be—in God's will for your life. Leaders are called to do what is right from God's perspective, not what the majority of the crowd votes on. Be bold, be courageous, and do it all in love toward others. They will respect you for following God.

CHALLENGE

Do you think about how certain people will react before you make a decision? Who are they? Has this perceived reaction affected your ability to obey the voice of God? What decisions do you have to make that requires the voice of the Lord over the voice of others?

ACTION

_____

_____

_____

_____

_____

DAY 30: PROVERBS 30

VERSE

Four things on earth are small, yet they are extremely wise: Ants are creatures of little strength, yet they store up their food in the summer; hyraxes are creatures of little power, yet they make their home in the crags; locusts have no king, yet they advance together in ranks; a lizard can be caught with the hand, yet it is found in kings' palaces. (Proverbs 30:24–28)

THOUGHT

Leaders are learners. They give attention to the details of their lives and try to learn from them. They are aware that there is a lesson to be learned in every situation and circumstance in life. They are not above learning from unconventional sources or things that would seem irrational. Leaders look for God's handprint on just about everything and gain wisdom through it all.

CHALLENGE

What areas of life have you been taking for granted and not learning from? How can you be more intentional about learning from everyone and everything everywhere?

ACTION

_____

_____

_____

_____

_____

DAY 31: PROVERBS 31

VERSE

Speak up for those who cannot speak for themselves, for the rights of all who are destitute. (Proverbs 31:8)

THOUGHT

Being a Christian leader carries great responsibility and privilege. When we lead, we get a chance to be the voice for those who cannot speak, to stand up for those who have fallen, to defend those who have no defense, to proclaim grace for those who sit in judgment, and to speak life for those who see death.

We are called to stand in the gap for people who are beaten up, rejected, wrongly treated, and forgotten. What an honor it is to model for others the same thing Jesus did for us when we were lost and broken. God is calling out to leaders across the world to stand up for justice and to proclaim victory for those who are in bondage all for Christ's glory.

CHALLENGE

What a great responsibility and privilege we have being leaders for Christ. How can you stand up for someone who is currently knocked down?

ACTION

_____

_____

_____

_____

_____

MONTH 2

DAY 1: PROVERBS 1

VERSE

My son, if sinful men entice you, do not give in to them. My son, do not go along with them, do not set foot on their paths. (Proverbs 1:10, 15)

THOUGHT

If you are a parent, you have probably told your child something similar to the above verses. "Son, if those kids are getting into trouble, don't follow them." As adults, we often get caught up in the same antics, trying to avoid sin and not give into the temptation of ungodly people. Even though this is extremely wise advice, I'm not convinced simply avoiding sin is the best approach. In fact, if we become more God-focused in our thoughts rather than worrying about temptation, it becomes much easier to turn down the enticement of sin. Leaders will then find themselves chasing after the Holy Spirit, rather than running away from sinner's enticement. Chasing someone is a lot more fun and effective than running away from something.

CHALLENGE

Do you find yourself running away from ungodly people? Are you constantly worried about how to avoid sin instead of how to follow the Holy Spirit? How can you renew your mind today (Romans 12:2) and begin chasing after God rather than getting caught up in the enticement of sin? How will you become more God-focused and less sin-focused?

ACTION

_____

_____

_____

_____

_____

DAY 2: PROVERBS 2

VERSE

My son, if you accept my words and store up my commands within you…then you will understand the fear of the LORD and find the knowledge of God. (Proverbs 2:1, 5)

THOUGHT

There are additional instructions given in verses 2–4 that culminate with the listener understanding the fear of the Lord and finding the knowledge of God. The phrase "store up my commands within you" caught my attention the most. When a supermarket stocks up on groceries, the market must already possess the food. When I store my favorite songs on my iPod, I already own them. When someone stores a boat at the dock, the boat belongs to them, and they have access to it anytime. If any of these stored items are not used, they go to waste. As leaders, we would be wasting God's commands if we merely memorize them or print them on fancy stationery. I believe we must own them, possess them, and practice them regularly until they become part of our everyday living. Experiencing a biblical truth is the only way we can store it for ongoing access.

CHALLENGE

Are there commands, instructions, or promises you have memorized or learned from God's Word but never actually experienced in your life? Do you have knowledge about a biblical truth but never applied it in everyday situations? Choose one of the first thoughts God brings to mind and decide right now to step out and ask Him to activate it in your life today.

ACTION

_____

_____

_____

_____

_____

DAY 3: PROVERBS 3

VERSE

Do not accuse anyone for no reason—when they have you no harm. (Proverbs 3:30)

THOUGHT

Whether you are leading a business, a team of volunteers, or your children, you will regularly have the responsibility of hearing accusations of another person's behavior. As we listen, we must refrain from accusation. We are to lead people into restoration and healing, not into division and strife. The moment we accuse someone, we take away our right to minister to them. Accusation turns us into a prosecuting attorney rather than a loving shepherd. We can, and should, quietly go to them and show them their sin if, in fact, we have tangible proof that a sin has occurred. Until then, we use wisdom in listening to the complaints, praying for discernment, and moving toward restoration.

CHALLENGE

Is there someone you are now avoiding or are bitter toward because you have accused them of something? Did you talk to them face-to-face before making the accusation? Okay, did you talk to them face-to-face *after* making the accusation? What steps are you going to take today toward restoration and healing so you can once again have a positive influence in their life?

ACTION

_____

_____

_____

_____

_____

DAY 4: PROVERBS 4

VERSE

The path of the righteous is like the morning sun, shining ever brighter till the full light of day. But the way of the wicked is like deep darkness; they do not know what makes them stumble. (Proverbs 4:18, 19)

THOUGHT

It's good to have a flashlight when you're caught in the dark. Not only can you help yourself, you can also help others who need the light. When you take your role as a leader seriously and stay on the path of the righteous (the "way of wisdom" in verse 11), you will not only illuminate your own path, your light will also shine bright enough to help others stay on the right path. Make wise choices, live in purity, act with integrity, and people will follow you as your path shines brighter and brighter. You can then truly be the "light of the world" (Matthew 5:14) to people who desperately need direction in life.

CHALLENGE

How can you live with a greater awareness that your choices in life affect each person who follows you? Identify one or two areas on your path that are getting dimmer instead of brighter, and write what you are going to do about it today. Then remind yourself that you are the righteousness of God in Christ (2 Corinthians 5:21) and begin walking once again on the path God has called you to.

ACTION

_____

_____

_____

_____

_____

DAY 5: PROVERBS 5

VERSE

May your fountain be blessed, and may you rejoice in the wife of your youth. Why, my son, be intoxicated with another man's wife? Why embrace the bosom of a wayward woman? (Proverbs 5:18, 20)

THOUGHT

The grass is not always greener on the other side. In fact, the grass is never greener on the other side if it isn't the grass God has given to you. I see two concepts in these verses that expand beyond marriage. The first one is rejoicing. Leaders know how to celebrate what God is doing in their life and rejoice over what God has given them. It's the secret to contentment. The second is being captivated. You are captivated by whatever has your attention. If you don't learn to celebrate and rejoice over what God is doing for you, and giving to you, you will most definitely be captivated by a counterfeit. Counterfeits look good, and they feel good, but they *never* produce healthy results.

CHALLENGE

What are several things that God is doing in your life right now that you can celebrate? What are several blessings that God has given to you in the past that you can rejoice over? How can you make celebration and rejoicing a regular part of your daily interaction with God?

ACTION

_____

_____

_____

_____

_____

DAY 6: PROVERBS 6

VERSE

If you have been trapped by what you said, ensnared by the words of your mouth, then do this, my son, to free yourself…go and humble yourself; press your plea with your neighbor! (Proverbs 6:2–3)

THOUGHT

Leaders are wise to quickly learn humility. A true act of humility is dying to yourself. Philippians 2:8 says Jesus "humbled Himself by becoming obedient to death—even death on a cross." When you die to yourself, you are no longer worried about how you appear to others when you fail, because you're already dead! When you are trapped by what you have said and you have messed up big time, you will be able to go and plea with the one you have failed. You will be willing to open your heart to them and become vulnerable to the point of humiliation as you ask for forgiveness. This type of humility will position you to receive protection and restoration from the Lord no matter the outcome of the conversation.

CHALLENGE

How willing are you to go and ask for forgiveness when you have failed someone? Do you stall, or do you handle it quickly? Do you make yourself vulnerable to them, or do you still hold back? Ask the Lord to reveal anything that is hindering true humility in your interaction with others and decide how you will give it over to the Lord today.

ACTION

_____

_____

_____

_____

_____

DAY 7: PROVERBS 7

VERSE

At the window of my house I looked out through the lattice. I saw among the simple, I noticed among the young men, a youth who had no sense. (Proverbs 7:6–7)

THOUGHT

The writer of this proverb explains in great detail what he observes starting in verse 6. Behaviors, schemes, and consequences are all noted. Observation is an extremely important element of leading others. It includes observing their surroundings and being aware of what may harm them and disrupt them from the Lord's mission. As a parent, I must observe the devil's schemes and train my children against them and toward the Lord. As a pastor, I must observe causes of burnout and motivate people to stay healthy. Take time to stop and observe your environment. Then use your findings to benefit your people and protect them from harm.

CHALLENGE

Who do you lead? Remember, leadership is influence. Whoever you influence, you lead. Whoever follows you or asks for your advice, you lead. How will you be more proactive in observing the environment they live, work, or serve in and then prayerfully share the things that may cause a roadblock for them? When will you do this?

ACTION

_____

_____

_____

_____

_____

DAY 8: PROVERBS 8

VERSE

Counsel and sound judgment are mine; I have insight, I have power. By me kings reign and rulers issue decrees that are just; by me princes govern, and all nobles—all who rule on earth. (Proverbs 8:14–16)

THOUGHT

Wisdom is the voice speaking in these verses. Two characteristics of wisdom are understanding and power. These characteristics equip kings, rulers, princes, and nobles to have proper dominion in their area of influence. Understanding and power also equip us to have proper dominion in our area of influence. The key is leading with them in balance. If there is an excess of understanding, there will be empathy, insight, and counsel but no empowerment to provide lasting solutions. If there is an excess of power, people will be taken advantage of and used for the benefit of the ruler. With both in balance, a leader will have proper perspective, along with the authority to make lasting change.

CHALLENGE

Think about the last three conversations with others whom you influence. Which of these two characteristics do you lead with more often, understanding or power? What will you ask the Lord to do in your life that will help bring balance in these two areas?

ACTION

_____

_____

_____

_____

_____

DAY 9: PROVERBS 9

VERSE

If you are wise, your wisdom will reward you; if you are a mocker, you alone will suffer. (Proverbs 9:12)

THOUGHT

Good leadership starts with good self-management. Being wise stewards of our own life has benefits of its own. These benefits or rewards can be enjoyed because God loves you and wants to see you fulfilled. He is not a slave driver who forces you to be wise only to benefit everyone else around you. No, God has given you the choice to be wise through the Holy Spirit so He can delight in you. These benefits overflow to those who surround you, but realize first that He rewards those (you) who earnestly seek Him (Hebrews 11:6). In His presence, there is wisdom. In wisdom, there is reward.

CHALLENGE

Are you trying too hard to be a good leader instead of first spending time in God's presence to receive divine wisdom? Identify several ways in which you are striving instead of allowing God to do His work through you. How will you earnestly seek Him today?

ACTION

_____

_____

_____

_____

_____

DAY 10: PROVERBS 10

VERSE

The name of the righteous is used in blessings, but the name of the wicked will rot. (Proverbs 10:7)

THOUGHT

Good leaders do not just create memories. They create legacies. The phrase "memory of the righteous" in verse 7 speaks more of a lasting, impactful heritage rather than happy thoughts about a person. A legacy impacts lives for generations to come. Memories become stories that are told around campfires. The best way a leader can be remembered is by the difference that remains in a culture (church, business, home, etc.) years after they have passed away. We should be much more concerned about how people will live differently because of our leadership rather than what stories they will tell about us someday.

CHALLENGE

Are you creating nice memories that will become nostalgic stories, or are you creating a lasting legacy that will impact your great-great-great-grandchildren? What can you change about your leadership that will create this type of legacy?

ACTION

_____

_____

_____

_____

_____

DAY 11: PROVERBS 11

VERSE

For lack of guidance a nation falls, victory is won through many advisers. (Proverbs 11:14)

THOUGHT

I have heard it said that a leader is only as strong as those who surround him/her. Though this principle is evident in verse 14 in regards to nations, I am sure we can apply it to our own lives. Personal breakthrough and personal encounter with God is a necessity, so is surrounding yourself with others who have also experienced breakthrough and encounters with God. No matter how mature of a Christian you are, you still make decisions with your own filters and lenses. The wise people surrounding you will be able to supply the advice, guidance, reassurance, and encouragement that will help you live in victory with Christ.

CHALLENGE

Imagine being able to pick your own all-star advisory team, which would surround you to help you live in victory. Who would you pick (hint: they should still be alive)? If you are already in relationship with some of them, how can you give them more room in your heart as an advisor? If you have never met some of your top picks, what can you do to learn from their wisdom? Who knows, maybe you will have the chance to talk face-to-face with one of your heroes!

ACTION

_____

_____

_____

_____

_____

DAY 12: PROVERBS 12

VERSE

Anxiety weighs down the heart, but a kind word cheers it up. (Proverbs 12:25)

THOUGHT

We may have anxious hearts from time to time, yet anxiety and fear is not the will of the Lord for us. Yesterday you read about surrounding yourself with people who can help you live in victory. If this team is in place, then you will be cheered up when you get weighed down so you can position yourself as the kind-word giver in everybody else's life. Just think how many people would be happy in your sphere of influence if you were free to focus on giving kind words to all who looked discouraged. Have you ever interacted with a grumpy neighbor or coworker who changed his entire demeanor simply because you spoke an encouraging word? Your world is full of grumpy people who Jesus is commanding you to love as you do yourself.

CHALLENGE

Be intentional about speaking kind words to others until it becomes part of your lifestyle. Think of the most anxious or fearful person in your life right now. How will you encourage them today? When will you do this?

ACTION

_____

_____

_____

_____

_____

DAY 13: PROVERBS 13

VERSE

Wise people think before they act; fools don't—
and even brag about their foolishness. (Proverbs
13:16, NLT)

THOUGHT

It would be too easy to place this verse in the context of
immediate actions, like thinking quickly on your feet or
breathing deeply so you don't lose your temper in the heat
of the moment. It includes this, but leaders are much more
strategic about the way they live rather than being in reaction mode all the time. We would be wise to think *way
before* we act and form nonnegotiables before difficulty
arrives so when the time comes to decide, we know exactly
what to do. Learn to allot time to just think, daydream, and
pray. As you do, God will give you visions for your life, core
values, and goals so that you can renew your mind as you
get on with your daily life.

CHALLENGE

Do you schedule time in your week to simply think, dream, and pray? When will you do this next? How will you eliminate all distractions so you truly have time to daydream with the Lord?

ACTION

_____

_____

_____

_____

_____

DAY 14: PROVERBS 14

VERSE

Laughter can conceal a heavy heart, but when the laughter ends, the grief remains. (Proverbs 14:13, NLT)

THOUGHT

Many Christians are fake when they are around other people. They put on the "Sunday smile," but deep inside they are hurting. This does no good because everyone else is then forced to fake it also because they don't want to be the one with problems. Society desperately needs authentic Christian leaders who are going to step up and be transparent. That doesn't mean dumping all your problems on your team, business, or staff. It means being okay with not having it together all the time. Relate to people when they are broken. Share your story of suffering and pain. If you're grieving, grieve. If you're sad, cry. If you're broken, ask for help. If you are wrong, admit it. Transparency is much harder than smiling and saying, "How are you today?

Good? Good!" But in the long run, people will respect you and find their own freedom in your authenticity.

CHALLENGE

How authentic are you? Do you wear a mask on Sunday or any other day of the week? How can you break out of this mentality and begin having transparency with others? What will your first step be today?

ACTION

_____

_____

_____

_____

_____

DAY 15: PROVERBS 15

VERSE

The eyes of the LORD are everywhere, keeping watch on the wicked and the good. (Proverbs 15:3)

THOUGHT

Many leaders are extremely driven and think their way is the only way to get things done. Because of this, we can begin micromanaging and watching every detail. On the other hand, progressive leaders trust their teams and release them into real responsibility. This type of leader isn't afraid if someone fails or makes a mistake. They believe in their people to make wise decisions and trust that they are the right person for the job. The next time you begin doubting the work ethic or daily decisions of a person, remind yourself that the eyes of the Lord are keeping watch on them and will bring revelation and correction where needed.

CHALLENGE

Do you trust that the Lord's eyes are watching those who follow you? Do you believe that the Lord has everything under His care and will guide those who are following Him? What is one project or task that you are micromanaging right now? What could be the reasons you do not fully trust the person responsible for it? What practical steps can you take to trust him/her more and allow the Lord to keep watch?

ACTION

_____

_____

_____

_____

_____

DAY 16: PROVERBS 16

VERSE

The appetite of laborers works for them; their hunger drives them on. (Proverbs 16:26)

THOUGHT

It is common to get hungry for the type of food you are thinking about. As you eat this food, your desire for more of it grows. As you feed your desire, an appetite develops. An appetite that is fed consistently turns into a passion. For me, it's chocolate! For others, it's fruits or vegetables. For leaders, it should be the presence of God and the vision God has given for your life. We need to set our mind on these things, digest the promises over our life, desire more of God's presence, develop an appetite for encountering more of the Lord, and live in a passionate pursuit of the divine assignments God has given us on this side of eternity.

CHALLENGE

What currently drives you in your daily labor? Is it fear of failure? Is it anxiety over deadlines? Is it money? Take time today to identify what your major areas of responsibility are and what keeps you moving forward. Ask the Lord to reveal His vision for each area and begin to feed yourself on the Lord and His promises. What does it mean to you to feed yourself on the Lord? How will you approach this?

ACTION

_____

_____

_____

_____

_____

DAY 17: PROVERBS 17

VERSE

Whoever mocks the poor shows contempt for their Maker; whoever gloats over disaster will not go unpunished. (Proverbs 17:5)

THOUGHT

This verse gives a stern warning about gloating over disaster. To gloat means to glory, revel, or rejoice in something. Sometimes we think we are acting righteously when we condemn a high-level leader who has fallen, or denounce a godless nation when a natural disaster occurs, or criticize a family member when they reap the bad fruit that they have been sowing. To the proud, it looks like righteous anger. To the wise, it looks like gloating. Christians have a message of reconciliation, not judgment. We should put ourselves in a position, while staying true to our beliefs and values, to reconcile people to God and people to people. If we take a stance that alienates us from those who have suffered a disaster (physical, spiritual, emotional, etc.), then we will not be able to help with the restoration process.

CHALLENGE

Are you sometimes glad deep down inside when a person, business, or nation that you don't like faces disaster? Do you find yourself joining the media in publically condemning those who have fallen? How can you position yourself as a messenger of reconciliation rather than judgment? Who is one person you have recently criticized that you can reach out to today? How will reach out to them?

ACTION

_____

_____

_____

_____

_____

DAY 18: PROVERBS 18

VERSE

Fools find no pleasure in understanding but delight in airing their own opinions. (Proverbs 18:2)

THOUGHT

Have you ever been in a meeting where you were the one who was supposed to share an idea, strategy, or new approach to something, and the other person ended up monopolizing the conversation with their own ideas and opinions? You probably didn't feel valued or understood in the end. Leaders should constantly seek to understand the people they serve and work with. That involves talking less and listening more. It also involves asking good questions to get to the root of their thoughts, beliefs, and behaviors. The more we listen, discern, question, and understand up front, the more our opinion will be valued when we feel it is the best time to share. When people want advice, they will ask for it. All other times, seek to understand and keep your opinions to yourself.

CHALLENGE

Think through the last three days and revisit each conversation you had with people you influence. Who did most of the talking? Did you come away with a greater understanding of who they are and why they do what they do? Are you more equipped to serve them afterward? How will you approach your conversations differently today in such a way that you will seek to understand rather than share your opinion?

ACTION

_____

_____

_____

_____

_____

DAY 19: PROVERBS 19

VERSE

Desire without knowledge is not good—how much more will hasty feet miss the way! (Proverbs 19:2)

THOUGHT

I am blessed to meet regularly with a leader who is fully committed to the supernatural as much as he is fully committed to the practical. I have learned that both zeal and knowledge are needed. It's the ability to pray for the sick and expect an immediate healing while giving warm hospitality later that evening to house guests. It's fasting and praying for a large financial miracle while still making sure your electric bill is paid on time. We can pursue both zeal and knowledge with our entire heart and see both fully developed in our life. I believe the proper stewardship of the practical is what proves our trustworthiness in the supernatural. For example, if I honor the poor by giving them clothes and food, then I can be trusted to honor the demonized when they come for deliverance.

CHALLENGE

Are you fully committed to both zeal and knowledge? How do you demonstrate value for both the supernatural and practical? Is welcoming a new guest in your church as important as seeing someone come to Christ? Pray for one supernatural need you are aware of that will need divine intervention from God. Be willing to be part of God's answer to that prayer. Also, do something practical for someone in need today, expanding your ability to influence in both realms.

ACTION

_____

_____

_____

_____

_____

DAY 20: PROVERBS 20

VERSE

Do not say, "I'll pay you back for this wrong!" Wait for the LORD, and he will avenge you. (Proverbs 20:22)

THOUGHT

If you're normal, you don't like to be wronged by someone else. When you are wronged, you often want to pay the person back. Your maturity as a leader can be measured by your ability to not defend yourself by allowing the Lord to deliver you during times of attack. There are times that explanations are needed to protect your character and reputation. However, most offenses we face are unworthy of a response and only put us in the low position of the attacker when we retaliate. Most attackers are not looking to prove you wrong; they are looking for a fight by taking their anger out on you. Make a decision now to withhold retaliation until you have spoken to the Lord about it, as well as to one or two trusted friends, if needed. One lesson I have learned is to wait at least twenty-four hours before responding to an emotionally charged e-mail.

CHALLENGE

Do you find yourself wanting to pay people back when they wrong you, or do you quickly hand it over to God? Do you secretly scheme how you can vindicate yourself or truly allow the Lord to bring deliverance and victory? The last time that someone offended you, how did you react? Looking back, was there something you wished you did or didn't do? How will you respond the next time someone falsely accuses you or offends you?

ACTION

_____

_____

_____

_____

_____

DAY 21: PROVERBS 21

VERSE

In the LORD's hand the king's heart is a stream of water that he channels toward all who please him. (Proverbs 21:1)

THOUGHT

Being led by the Holy Spirit and staying flexible are important qualities for all Christians, especially those in leadership. We set goals, write agendas, accomplish tasks, and perform many other responsibilities. All this must take place in the context of being Spirit-led. Allow the Lord to direct your heart and life like a free-flowing river. Not only is it a more exciting way to live, it is also more fruit-bearing and beneficial to those around you since you are accomplishing the Lord's agenda more often than your own. In fact, the longer you are led by the Spirit, the more your agenda will mirror His. My mother always told me to stay flexible so I don't get bent out of shape. That rings true when following the Holy Spirit also. Be flexible, flow with His voice, and enjoy the ride!

CHALLENGE

How can you set your priorities and tasks to allow the Lord to direct you wherever He pleases? How can you structure your day so that divine interruptions won't ruin your plans or attitude? How can you become more Spirit-led?

ACTION

DAY 22: PROVERBS 22

VERSE

Do not move an ancient boundary stone set up by
your ancestors. (Proverbs 22:28)

THOUGHT

Receiving an inheritance, both spiritual and physical, is one
of the greatest honors an upcoming generation can receive.
In this context, portions of land were given to fathers by
God to steward for future generations. An inheritance
was designed to allow us to build upon the breakthroughs
of our forefathers. In essence, their ceiling of growth and
experience is to become our floor. Unfortunately, a spirit of
independence poisons some young leaders that think they
have to recreate anything that is effective and fruitful. They
end up moving boundaries, dishonoring the work of fathers
of the faith, and cut themselves off from the blessing. No
matter how old or young you are, it would be wise to honor
and value what has been passed down through the history
of the church and not try to move the boundaries God
intended us to live within.

CHALLENGE

How can you be more intentional and active about honoring previous generations of revival and breakthrough? Read Matthew 10:41–42 and ask the Lord to show you the specific anointings, breakthroughs, and mantles that have been evident in your ancestry, church, or city. What is one way you can begin building upon that today?

ACTION

_____

_____

_____

_____

_____

DAY 23: PROVERBS 23

VERSE

My son, if your heart is wise, then my heart will be glad indeed; my inmost being will rejoice when your lips speak what is right. (Proverbs 23:15–16)

THOUGHT

Without even being aware of it, people usually lead with either a brotherhood or fatherhood mentality. (Women lead with sisterhood or motherhood, of course). Brothers compete and fight to be the fastest, strongest, and smartest. It is hard for a brother to be glad and rejoice when the other experiences major success since it threatens their own progress. On the other hand, fathers do not compete against sons but invest all they have to raise them up for greatest effectiveness. Fathers can truly celebrate the victories of their sons and rejoice in their inmost being when they see their son walking in righteousness. One mentality of leading creates bitterness, the other true joy.

CHALLENGE

Discern which style of leadership you are operating with. Is your heart glad when those who follow you have great success? Can you easily rejoice when your team members surpass your own skill level? How can you lead more like a father or mother and eliminate all competition between you and those you influence?

ACTION

DAY 24: PROVERBS 24

VERSE

By wisdom a house is built, and through understanding it is established; through knowledge its rooms are filled with rare and beautiful treasures. (Proverbs 24:3–4)

THOUGHT

These verses have implications both physically and spiritually. Since most of us don't build our own houses anymore, we can focus solely on the spiritual. Leaders have the great responsibility of building a culture with those they influence. A culture is the desired beliefs, customs, practices, and social behavior of a particular group. If we are not intentional about building a desired culture, then the circumstances that our people find themselves in will build the culture for us. Wisdom lays the foundation for any culture. It determines the how and when. Understanding establishes the core values that people learn to live by and the boundaries in which they can take risk. Knowledge of what the Spirit is doing and how we as a people are to respond will fill the culture with rare and beautiful treasures. I consider these to be the blessing, favor, and manifest presence of His love and power.

CHALLENGE

What type of culture are you building with those who you influence? What core values have you established? Take time today to write a paragraph describing the desired beliefs, customs, practices, and social behavior of your people. Then decide on the first two steps toward creating that culture.

ACTION

_____

_____

_____

_____

_____

DAY 25: PROVERBS 25

VERSE

It is the glory of God to conceal a matter; to search out a matter is the glory of kings. (Proverbs 25:2)

THOUGHT

The Bible has levels of truth within it. For example, it is true that all believers are servants of God. It is also true that we are friends of God. Again, it is true that we are sons/daughters of God. These truths were revealed by Jesus and Paul throughout the New Testament during different stages of their teaching. I'm not sure how Paul received his enlightenment about our relationship with God, but I would argue that it did not all come at once but as progressive revelation. God's Word is full of truths that are easy to spot at first glance. It is also full of truths that are concealed by God to be searched out by His children. I'm not talking about some hidden code where the first letters of each sentence spell out a secret message. I simply believe God has deeper revelation for the children who are willing to meditate on His Word and open their hearts to receive the message of instruction He has for them that day.

CHALLENGE

Have you ever had that moment when you are reading a portion of Scripture you have read many times, and a light bulb goes off when you realize you just learned something new that you had never seen in that passage before? This is personal revelation that God has given you into another level of truth within His Word. How will you approach Scripture more intentionally to search out the matters that are concealed for His glory?

ACTION

_____

_____

_____

_____

_____

DAY 26: PROVERBS 26

VERSE

Do not answer a fool according to his folly, or you yourself will be just like him. Answer a fool according to his folly, or he will be wise in his own eyes. (Proverbs 26:4–5)

THOUGHT

These verses may confuse someone looking to deal with conflict in a clear and concise manner. We all know conflicts and arguments can be extremely complicated. Discernment is a huge component for leadership. If you apply verse 4 to all interaction with foolish people, they may end up leading other people astray since no one ever confronted them with the truth. If you apply verse 5 to all interaction with them, then you would bring yourself down to their level and look like a fool yourself. The solution is to discern when to keep quiet and when to confront. At times, we allow the foolish to argue their insignificant matters without responding. Other times, we confront the individual so he, along with all who hear, will know the truth and not be deceived. Both are correct ways to approach a situation. It's your responsibility to discern how the Lord is leading in that specific moment.

CHALLENGE

Do you have a tendency to keep quiet or confront when dealing with foolish and argumentative people? What are some questions you can ask the Lord during these moments that will help you discern the correct action?

ACTION

_____

_____

_____

_____

_____

DAY 27: PROVERBS 27

VERSE

If a man loudly blesses his neighbor early in the morning, it will be taken as a curse. (Proverbs 27:14)

THOUGHT

If you are not a morning person, then you totally understand this verse. Our words are extremely important. Giving words of life and encouragement is one of the most effective ways to build up others. Not only are the words we say important, but how, when, and why we say them are just as important. Most of us have experienced a time when we said something that was kind and encouraging but was taken as an insult. You may have wondered why it wasn't received well, only to later realize that the Spirit wasn't breathing those words at that moment. A right word at the wrong time can be worse than no word at all. We can't back down from giving daily encouragement to those we influence, but we need to be sensitive to the how, when, and why of our words for them to be anointed and effective.

CHALLENGE

Do you encourage people with the awareness of what the Holy Spirit is trying to say through you at that moment, or do you rely more on your own thoughts and emotions? Identify one incident when you tried to say something positive, but it was taken negatively. How can you approach this same situation differently in the future?

ACTION

_____

_____

_____

_____

_____

DAY 28: PROVERBS 28

VERSE

Those who work their land will have abundant food, but those who chase fantasies will have their fill of poverty. (Proverbs 28:19)

THOUGHT

I love hearing the dreams of other people. These dreams are rarely attainable with human strength and wisdom but need God to intervene in a major way. We see throughout the Bible men and women who had a God-given dream in front of them that gave their life vision and purpose. You will also notice that they didn't chase the dream or fantasy and leave productivity behind. Each one of us who has a God-given dream must grow where we are already planted, do well with what God has already given us, and faithfully steward the talents that are already in our hands. Dreams are obtained as part of a journey, with many steps and stages along the way. Work the land you are currently living on while keeping the dream God has given you alive in your heart. You will never get there (your dream) without first being effective here (your current season).

CHALLENGE

What is the dream God has given for your life? If you can't identify a dream, what are some significant accomplishments you feel God wants to do through you? How can you "work your land" in the season God has you in now that will help you eventually fulfill something greater?

ACTION

_____

_____

_____

_____

_____

DAY 29: PROVERBS 29

VERSE

Pride brings a person low, but the lowly in spirit gain honor. (Proverbs 29:23)

THOUGHT

God's kingdom operates opposite of the world's ways. In the world, people think self-pride positions you for promotion since it is a sign of strength and confidence. A lowly spirit would be frowned upon since it is a sign of weakness and lack. In God's kingdom, pride causes a man to fall and strips him from any recognition he deserves. A lowly spirit leads to a man being honored and recognized for His God-given gifts and talents. If you would like honor attributed to your name and reputation, which would in turn give honor to your Maker and King, it would be wise to check the attitude of your spirit and the motives of your good works.

CHALLENGE

Do you find yourself getting caught up living by the world's values instead of God's values? If so, which values challenge you the most? Think of the good works you did this past week and identify the attitude of your spirit and the motives that led you to these work. What do you need to adjust so that honor may be given to you and to your Father?

ACTION

_____

_____

_____

_____

_____

DAY 30: PROVERBS 30

VERSE

There are three things that are too amazing for me,
four that I do not understand: the way of an eagle
in the sky, the way of a snake on a rock, the way of a
ship on the high seas, and the way of a man with a
young woman. (Proverbs 30:18–19)

THOUGHT

Leadership, especially for those who oversee many people
and teams, can be very demanding and task-driven. Time
lines and deadlines are constantly looking over our shoul-
der, and much work must be accomplished each day. In the
midst of the intensity, it is vital that we take time to still
be amazed at the simple workings of God. It is refreshing
to watch a bird soar through the air. It brings awe to look
out over the horizon of water at the ocean. When we hold
an infant and examine his toes and eyelashes, it reminds
us of God's attention to detail. We can get so caught up in
our schedules that we forget how awesome God is unless

we intentionally take the time to once again be amazed by Him.

CHALLENGE

Stop three different times today for one minute each time and observe something in nature. Look at a piece of artwork or browse through a *National Geographic* magazine or website. Before the end of your day, journal what amazes you about God.

ACTION

_____

_____

_____

_____

_____

DAY 31: PROVERBS 31

VERSE

Her husband has full confidence in her and lacks nothing of value. (Proverbs 31:11)

THOUGHT

The majority of Proverbs 31 discusses a wife of noble character. Though her character and righteousness can be attributed to God and her response to what God is doing in her life, I thought verse 11 was interesting. Our confidence in others empowers them to be who God created them to be and to truly shine. Allowing others to thrive in their God-given potential also has a reciprocal effect on those who lead them. Our full confidence in who, or what, we lead will result in value being added back to us as leaders and to the organizations we lead.

CHALLENGE

How can you communicate the confidence you have in those who you lead? How can you build them up each day and speak to their value as God's child? What are you going to do differently today in this area?

ACTION

_____

_____

_____

_____

_____

MONTH 3

DAY 1: PROVERBS 1

VERSE

The proverbs of Solomon son of David, king of Israel. (Proverbs 1:1)

THOUGHT

Many readers will skim past this verse since it appears to be a simple introduction. However, this one verse actually reveals identity, heritage, legacy, and calling. The phrase "the proverbs of Solomon" shows that he had his own individual identity from God, and so do you. You need to realize that you are a unique masterpiece, and never again will God create someone exactly like you. Solomon was also the "son of David," which identifies the heritage which he came from and the legacy that he will pass on. Honoring those who have come before us (our heritage) by creating an environment of blessing for those who come after us (our legacy) is a sign of great wisdom. "King of Israel" was Solomon's calling by God. If we know who we are in Christ, where we have come from, and who is coming after us, then fulfilling God's calling in our life will make all the difference in the world.

CHALLENGE

Ask the Lord this question, "Who am I in You?" Take a few minutes to write down the thoughts and impressions you receive. Next, write down the names of people from previous generations, whether relatives or not, who have positively impacted your life. Now write names of people in future generations, whether relatives or not, whose lives you are currently impacting. Finally, ask God to define what He is calling you to do in this season of your life. After you write some ideas down, try to summarize these thoughts in one or two sentences.

ACTION

_____

_____

_____

_____

_____

DAY 2: PROVERBS 2

VERSE

For the upright will live in the land, and the blameless will remain in it. (Proverbs 2:21)

THOUGHT

Leaders understand the difference between God's favor and personal responsibility. God's favor is what establishes you as upright in your place of influence, but your blamelessness is what keeps you there. His favor gives you a place to "live in the land" since you are God's child and He is pleased to give you His kingdom. While God's favor establishes you, your integrity and character will keep you there to "remain in it." Not from a work of the flesh but through grace, you will be empowered to take responsibility of the favor you have been given, and as a result, you will remain in your sphere of influence. It's one thing to live in the land for a little while. It's another to remain in it and make a lasting impact.

CHALLENGE

Do you know the areas of life in which God has given you favor? List as many situations as you can from the past month where you have sensed God's favor resting upon you. Now circle the situations that you operated blamelessly in. Identify ways you could have taken more responsibility for the situations you did not circle and ask God to empower you to steward His favor more wisely next time.

ACTION

_____

_____

_____

_____

_____

DAY 3: PROVERBS 3

VERSE

Trust in the LORD with all your heart and lean not on your own understanding. (Proverbs 3:5)

THOUGHT

One of the most honest answers a leader can give when asked why God has done or has not done something in a person's life is, "I don't know." God's Word tells us to trust in the Lord with our heart. When we trust Him entirely, we give up our right to understand everything that is going on. We also give up our right to have an answer for every question. Instead of trying to come up with a logical conclusion, just trust Him. If we know for sure that He is a good God and there is never lack on His end, then we will be able to live in mystery while not blaming God for the bad stuff.

CHALLENGE

While we are to seek knowledge, understanding, and wisdom, some things in life will still remain a mystery. List several mysteries in your life right now, things you wish you had an answer for but simply do not. Ask the Lord if you are blaming Him for any of these things and repent if you are. What can you do differently today that demonstrates a greater trust in God?

ACTION

_____

_____

_____

_____

_____

DAY 4: PROVERBS 4

VERSE

For I, too, was once my father's son, tenderly loved.... My father taught me, "Take my words to heart.... Get wisdom; develop good judgment. Don't forget my words or turn away from them." (Proverbs 4:3–5, NLT)

THOUGHT

Solomon gives us a glimpse of David's teaching and discipleship of him while Solomon was still young. In 1 Kings 3:5–15, we see the result of David's discipleship when Solomon asks God for wisdom and understanding. I believe Solomon prayed for wisdom because his father instructed him to seek it from a very young age. Our current discipleship is forming the prayers of future generations. What we teach younger generations and how we teach it will directly impact what they pray and how they pray it in the years to come. What an awesome privilege we have—to be able to affect someone's life, knowing that what we give them may become a pivotal prayer decades later.

CHALLENGE

How has the instruction you received as a child affected your prayers as an adult? Write out a few specific prayers you would want someone that you are currently influencing to pray in future years. Develop a simple but clear plan on how you will instruct them toward these prayers in the next month.

ACTION

_____

_____

_____

_____

_____

DAY 5: PROVERBS 5

VERSE

Keep to a path far from her [an adulteress]…lest you lose your honor to others and your dignity to one who is cruel, lest strangers feast on your wealth and your toil enrich the house of another. At the end of your life you will groan, when your flesh and body are spent. (Proverbs 5:8–11)

THOUGHT

Jesus taught that we are given different amounts of gifts, money, talents, etc., to steward during our life. One day, we will return to the Father taking nothing with us. Our lives and resources are on a timetable, and we get to choose how to spend them. We must choose to give our strength, years, and resources to people and projects that have value and are worth the investment. At the same time, we must be intentional about avoiding the paths that will waste our strength, years, and resources. The difference will be ending our race strong or ending it depleted.

CHALLENGE

Identify one or two people and one or two projects that are worth investing much of your time, energy, strength, money, and resources into. Write down several ways you can begin investing in these people and projects this week.

ACTION

_____

_____

_____

_____

_____

DAY 6: PROVERBS 6

VERSE

Can a man scoop fire into his lap without his clothes being burned? Can a man walk on hot coals without his feet being scorched? (Proverbs 6:27–28)

THOUGHT

If you play with fire, you will get burned. No one is above the natural consequences of sin, not business leaders, parents, elders, deacons, or ministers. Leadership often comes with privileges, whether in the home, office, or church, but we can't take those privileges for granted. For example, I am the leader in my home, so I can choose to eat as much dessert as I want whenever I want. But being the leader won't stop my body from expanding at an unhealthy rate! No matter what position of influence you have, sin is still sin, and you will suffer the consequences. Are you forgiven? Yes. Does God still love you? Yes. Does His grace and mercy remove all eternal punishment from the Father? Yes. Do natural consequences still exist on this earth? Yes.

CHALLENGE

Are you currently playing with fire in any area of your life? Are you living in intentional disobedience toward God? If so, go to the Lord in prayer right now and confess this disobedience. Ask Him to remove any temptation to rekindle that fire in the future and begin walking in the Spirit so you will not satisfy the desires of your flesh.

ACTION

_____

_____

_____

_____

_____

DAY 7: PROVERBS 7

VERSE

Say to wisdom, "You are my sister," and to insight, "You are my relative." (Proverbs 7:4)

THOUGHT

I think most Christian leaders would admit to having some measure of wisdom and understanding. However, it takes an acute awareness of this wisdom to implement it properly in difficult situations. I love the analogy this verse gives to wisdom and understanding being our sister, brother, or relative. Growing up, I always knew I had an older sister who loved me, whether she was with me at the time or not. However, when a difficult situation came and I was acutely aware that she was right next to me, things were a lot less scary since I knew she would stand up for me. Don't settle for simply knowing you have wisdom, but be aware that it (and God) is present with you at that specific moment of difficulty.

CHALLENGE

Do you look at wisdom as unrelated principles that you can't practically apply in life's difficult situations? Do you have a hard time relying on the wisdom of God when things get rough for you? Jot down the last few difficult situations you encountered and how you responded. Ask God to reveal whether you were operating in godly wisdom. Now ask Him to give you the ability to become acutely aware of His wisdom at all times and in all situations.

ACTION

DAY 8: PROVERBS 8

VERSE

I [wisdom] was there when he set the heavens in place, when he marked out the horizon on the face of the deep. (Proverbs 8:27)

THOUGHT

It is hard to fathom that the same knowledge, good judgment, and sound decision-making ability that God used to set the heavens in place and mark out the horizon now resides in us. How many times as leaders do we make decisions based on our own judgments or calculations without first relying on the wisdom that figured out where the stars and galaxies were going to settle? I can use my own thirty-some years of personal experience, or I can use the wisdom that carved the shape of the earth. If God figured out how gravity can keep us attached to the earth while it spins at approximately 1,038 miles per hour, then He can surely figure out how to handle a person who is causing conflict in your business, neighborhood, school, or ministry.

CHALLENGE

This might seem like an odd challenge, but take the next thirty minutes and search for some statistics on the Internet. Of course, check several sites for accuracy. Search things like, "How many stars exist?" and "How far away is the nearest galaxy?" Take time to simply be amazed at God's creation and how much of it we will never even see. As we gain perspective on how wise and immense He is, it will make our tough decisions seem like easy work for Him.

ACTION

_____

_____

_____

_____

_____

DAY 9: PROVERBS 9

VERSE

Stolen water is sweet; food eaten in secret is delicious. (Proverbs 9:17)

THOUGHT

There is something about the rush and excitement of mischievousness that makes it appealing to those on a long journey of growth. It's the feeling many teenagers get when they take their first drink of alcohol behind their parents' shed or when a young couple sneak a kiss behind the teacher's back. Spiritual growth is a lifelong journey that takes time to develop, and it has no shortcuts or gimmicks. Leaders have the opportunity to decline a momentary rush of immorality for the consistent increase of God's anointing on their lives. It may not be easy, but it is worth it in the end.

CHALLENGE

Recall a time in your life when you secretly did something that was wrong. How did it make you feel while you were doing it? How did you feel afterward? Was it worth it? How does this apply to your life as a follower of Jesus?

ACTION

_____

_____

_____

_____

_____

DAY 10: PROVERBS 10

VERSE

Whoever walks in integrity walks securely, but whoever takes crooked paths will be found out. (Proverbs 10:9)

THOUGHT

When we submit ourselves to the grace of God and allow integrity to be developed in our lives, we can walk daily with the confidence and security that we are pleasing God, no matter what man may think. It won't matter if we receive false accusations, slander, or insults. Knowing that we are walking in integrity allows for total transparency and vulnerability without the risk of losing reputation in man's eyes. We don't have to look around with shifty eyes, being paranoid of the next verbal attack. When we live with an audience of One, our integrity will keep us strong and whole, even when people have the wrong impression of us.

CHALLENGE

Integrity is much more than just a defense against people who slander us. Integrity is absolutely necessary to be able to properly handle an attack when it comes. Ask God to show you areas in your life that are strong with integrity and write them down.

ACTION

_____

_____

_____

_____

_____

DAY 11: PROVERBS 11

VERSE

Like a gold ring in a pig's snout is a beautiful woman
who shows no discretion. (Proverbs 11:22)

THOUGHT

This verse is such a good reminder to just be yourself and
not try to put on the appearance of something greater, or
you will end up looking like a muddy, sloppy pig with a
fancy piece of jewelry stuck in its nose. Titles, positions,
and statistics have infected the Christian world the same
way it has secular society. Some Christians make sure they
mention the size of their church, what leadership position they hold, or how much they gave to a certain charity.
In the end, you may be able to wear a fancy pin that says
"100% Sunday School Attendance," but if you still act like
a fool, guess what people will remember you by?

CHALLENGE

Take time to list the gifts and talents the Lord has given you. What are you doing to implement these gifts and talents into your everyday life? How can you better utilize them to simply be you—nothing more, nothing less?

ACTION

_____

_____

_____

_____

_____

DAY 12: PROVERBS 12

VERSE

Those who work their land will have abundant food, but those who chase fantasies have no sense. (Proverbs 12:11)

THOUGHT

If we want to see positive results in our lives, we need to work our own land. Identifying which land is ours to work is the first step. Avoiding chasing after fantasies (other people's land) is the next. It's healthy to have vision and God-given dreams, but chasing after fantasies will only result in failure. An example of this would be an owner of a restaurant taking much of his workday to imagine what it would be like to own a technology firm. He could potentially wish away several years of his career fantasizing what could be instead of working the land God has already given him. If God wants to transplant you into a new land, let Him do it in His timing and in His way. Until then, faithfully work your own land. And by the way, if you want the grass to be greener on your side, add some fertilizer.

CHALLENGE

Take a few minutes in prayer right now and ask the Lord to identify what "land" He has already given you to work. He might talk to you about your family, neighborhood, work-place, or something else. Write down what you feel He has shared with you and list two ways you can increase your effectiveness in each area.

ACTION

_____

_____

_____

_____

_____

DAY 13: PROVERBS 13

VERSE

Walk with the wise and become wise, for a companion of fools suffers harm. (Proverbs 13:20)

THOUGHT

If you acknowledge that you are leading others in one or several areas of your life, you should always try to improve the skills needed to lead them more effectively. One way to do that is to surround yourself with people who are already doing what you want to do better. If you want to grow in wisdom, hang out with wise people. If you want to parent better, hang out with great parents. If you want to steward your finances better, hang out with people who have paid off all their debt and are extremely generous. As you walk with these people, their strengths will rub off on you. As a result, you will be able to impart these skills to those you lead.

CHALLENGE

List several skills or areas of knowledge you want to improve. Now list people you already know, whether personally or through social networks, who are doing what you want to do. Write down three questions you can ask them to begin growing in these areas. Set a date for contacting each of these people to set up a meeting, a lunch, or an online discussion if distance is an issue.

ACTION

_____

_____

_____

_____

_____

DAY 14: PROVERBS 14

VERSE

Whoever is patient has great understanding, but one who is quick-tempered displays folly. (Proverbs 14:29)

THOUGHT

There is an obvious correlation between how patient someone is and how much understanding they gain. Patience allows for several things to occur that eventually lead to great understanding. Patience allows for both sides of a story to be told before a decision is made. Patience allows for the heart of the issue to be revealed instead of reacting to the surface issue. Patience allows for the one who is struggling to vent without feeling the need to argue or defend. Patience allows for prayer before a conclusion is made. Patience allows for the counsel of others when a determination can't be made alone. Patience allows for the blood pressure in all parties to decline before moving forward. Patience allows for our mouths to stay shut instead of saying something in the flesh rather than from the Spirit.

CHALLENGE

Identify two areas of your life where you are the most and the least patient. Ask the Lord why you are patient in some areas but not others. How is this impatience hurting your relationships? How can improved patience help you lead better?

ACTION

DAY 15: PROVERBS 15

VERSE

A person finds joy in giving an apt reply—and how good is a timely word! (Proverbs 15:23)

THOUGHT

I love Spirit-led conversations, where I give someone an answer to a difficult question and then think to myself, *Man, that was awesome advice!* It feels so good to nail a solid answer, doesn't it? At first, I used to feel bad about feeling so good after a conversation like this. Then I began to realize that I wasn't really the one speaking, so my joy was simply a response to how God spoke through me in spite of me. Now I just sit back and enjoy how good my answers sound during some (definitely not all) conversations and appreciate how God can use someone like me in such complex situations! It is such a privilege to speak life and encouragement to those in need at exactly the right time, as long as we are sensitive to when and how God wants it spoken.

CHALLENGE

No false humility here. Jot down several times in the recent past where you felt really good about an answer or advice that you gave someone. Try to recognize what it was that led to your answer or advice, and then spend time giving God thanks for using you to speak life to someone else.

ACTION

_____

_____

_____

_____

_____

DAY 16: PROVERBS 16

VERSE

Commit to the LORD whatever you do, and he will establish your plans. (Proverbs 16:3)

THOUGHT

Many people use a to-do list to accomplish daily tasks that support a larger project. Whether it's a home repair list or a business plan, our motives are most likely pure while developing these lists. However, what if we went a step further and had a daily briefing with the Lord and actually asked Him what He wanted us to accomplish today? I know that personally, I would be nervous that all my calls wouldn't get made or a certain task would miss its deadline. Seriously, would God send us in the wrong direction if we went to Him first and then developed our to-dos? I don't think so. Be reminded today that when we commit to the Lord in whatever we do, our plans will succeed!

CHALLENGE

Take the next five days and start with a blank agenda. Write a time and location where you will receive this briefing from the Lord. Spend several minutes in prayer discerning what He wants you to accomplish, then do those first. At the end of the five days, evaluate your success. You just might approach the rest of your life differently.

ACTION

DAY 17: PROVERBS 17

VERSE

Starting a quarrel is like breaching a dam; so drop the matter before a dispute breaks out. (Proverbs 17:14)

THOUGHT

What great imagery there is in this verse! Think about how many less quarrels you would start if you pictured a dam busting loose with the rushing waters of dispute pouring over you. It does leaders well to consider the consequences before pressing a matter too far. When you are sensing that a person is disconnecting with your suggestions or is getting irritated with your conversation, back off and commit it to prayer until the Lord opens another door for conversation. The last thing you want it to get drenched with their anger-filled words and potentially harm their trust in you. Learn to drop it and move on if the issue isn't an emergency or of top priority.

CHALLENGE

Write the name of the last person with whom you pressed a matter too far and began a dispute over something that was not very important. Record some reasons why you may have gone too far. Identify several ways you can avoid breaching that dam again.

ACTION

_____

_____

_____

_____

_____

DAY 18: PROVERBS 18

VERSE

The first to speak in court sounds right—until the cross-examination begins. (Proverbs 18:17)

THOUGHT

Whether you are leading your organization, ministry, or family, you will have plenty of opportunities to hear the case of someone who has been hurt or offended. And as you listen to the case being presented, allow the Holy Spirit to keep your mind open to what will be presented by the other person before you make a conclusion. There are two sides to every story. The second side of the story usually brings facts to the table that makes the first side more balanced and realistic. It can be so hard at times to just sit and listen without forming a conclusion, but it is a necessary skill for leaders to be effective reconcilers. The process may look like this: listen, take mental notes, listen to the other person, compare stories, ask God for wisdom, form a conclusion, and work toward reconciliation with both people.

CHALLENGE

Write the names down of the last people who came to you in a dispute with differing stories. How did you approach your gathering of information? What were strong points about your listening skills? How may you approach this differently in the future?

ACTION

_____

_____

_____

_____

_____

DAY 19: PROVERBS 19

VERSE

Penalties are prepared for mockers, and beatings for the backs of fools. (Proverbs 19:29)

THOUGHT

Verse 18 of this same Proverb discusses the benefits of disciplining a son. Verse 29 explains a different way of dealing with people using penalties and beatings. It will do you well to know the difference and decide which method you will use. The way you deal with people on a regular basis will determine the culture that is created within your area of influence. Discipline gets people who are off the path back on the path. Penalties and beatings cause wounded spirits and bodies to the ones who are off the path and do not show them a way back. To help you decide which method you should use, ask yourself this question, "Do I want sons and daughters or mockers and fools to be developed under my influence?"

CHALLENGE

How can you interact with people more effectively by using grace, mercy, and discipline rather than criticism, punishment, and beatings? What do you think some of the outcomes will be as a result of this?

ACTION

_____

_____

_____

_____

_____

DAY 20: PROVERBS 20

VERSE

Ears that hear and eyes that see—the LORD has made them both. (Proverbs 20:12)

THOUGHT

There are endless resources, including this book hopefully, for becoming a better leader. At times it will seem too complicated and complex as you follow a Savior who seemed much simpler. When all the principles, strategies, and insights block your ability to be the person God created you to be, it's time to simplify. Realize the simplicity of these two gifts from God—your ears and eyes. Remove yourself from all the checklists of leadership and take time to listen and look at your surroundings. Enjoy what God has given you. Use your senses to identify any needs that are present and simply serve.

CHALLENGE

How have your leadership responsibilities become too complicated and complex? What is the Lord saying to you about simplifying? When is the last time you just sat back for a few moments to look around and listen to your surroundings? Do it now, and record what the Lord shows you.

ACTION

_____

_____

_____

_____

_____

DAY 21: PROVERBS 21

VERSE

When justice is done, it brings joy to the righteous
but terror to evildoers. (Proverbs 21:15)

THOUGHT

I have been surprised at times by the reaction of others
when I feel a rational decision has been made but has
caused some to be happy and others very upset. I am once
again reminded that decisions of justice are bound to bring
mixed reaction. The response of others cannot dictate your
decisions, or those who have the strongest response will
influence your definition of justice. The Word of God, both
written and spoken, should be your defining factor, not how
happy or mad someone is going to be with you once your
decision is announced.

CHALLENGE

Do the potential reactions of specific people come to mind when you are deciding what is just and right? Who are they? Why do you think they come to mind? Ask the Lord to remove any fear of man you may have and to increase your fear of the Lord so your decisions can be sound and just at all times.

ACTION

_____

_____

_____

_____

_____

DAY 22: PROVERBS 22

VERSE

Rich and poor have this in common: The LORD is the Maker of them all. (Proverbs 22:2)

THOUGHT

Snowflakes are similar to people in that no two are exactly alike. From morning until evening, you probably interact with people who are vastly different from each other. Their age, race, ethnicity, social status, intelligence, and personality, just to name a few, are all unique. At the end of the day, we must realize that the Lord has created each one of them in His own image and knew them before they were ever known. Valuing each person we come in contact with, first and foremost, as being created by God, will drastically affect our attitude toward them. We will begin to see people as God sees them, not as society labels them.

CHALLENGE

Do you have a tendency to judge people based on their gender, age, intelligence, wealth, race, etc.? If so, explain how and what areas you show more partiality. How can you begin to see people as created in the image of God, rather than created in the image of social status?

ACTION

_____

_____

_____

_____

_____

DAY 23: PROVERBS 23

VERSE

Cast but a glance at riches, and they are gone, for they will surely sprout wings and fly off to the sky like an eagle. (Proverbs 23:5)

THOUGHT

There is nothing wrong with a person enjoying prosperity when it is accompanied by a godly purpose. Wealth and prosperity become a problem when our eyes are fixed on the temporal rather than the eternal. Wise leaders are intentional about investing in the eternal aspects of people's lives while meeting their temporal needs. As the eternal is brought into perspective, those who learn from us will keep their focus on God's unshakable kingdom, rather than money and things, which are temporary and fleeting. Jesus met the needs of people in both arenas, but it always pointed to an eternal truth about His Father's kingdom.

CHALLENGE

How are you using your financial resources to invest into God's kingdom? How are you guarding yourself against glancing too long at your temporal resources? What are you doing to invest into the eternal aspects of people who learn from you?

ACTION

_____

_____

_____

_____

_____

DAY 24: PROVERBS 24

VERSE

If you falter in times of trouble, how small is your strength! (Proverbs 24:10)

THOUGHT

A person's physical strength can only be measured by the amount of resistance placed against him or her. For example, no one is going to acknowledge the strength of a professional weight lifter if he bench presses pillows at a competition. In the same way, the strength of our faith and endurance can only be measured during times of resistance. During times of peace and rest, there is little that requires our spiritual muscles to flex. When trouble comes, the foundation of our relationship with the Lord and our confidence in His strength working through us are put to the test. It is in those difficult and dark times that the Lord will show off all that He has trained us to be. It is our responsibility to submit to these trainings before the trouble comes, or our strength will look small in the end.

CHALLENGE

First, be honest with yourself by acknowledging whose strength you are operating in during trouble, yours or the Lord's? Write down the last two situations that have caused resistance. How did you react? What was the result? What will you do now to train for future problems?

ACTION

_____

_____

_____

_____

_____

DAY 25: PROVERBS 25

VERSE

Like clouds and wind without rain is one who boasts of gifts never given. (Proverbs 25:14)

THOUGHT

I can still remember sitting in my bedroom with a friend while trading baseball cards. He swore he had a real Babe Ruth card in his parent's car and was willing to trade it for a player who was good, not even great. As he went out to get the card, my anticipation, hope, and excitement rose by the second. To my dismay, this Babe Ruth card was a sketched image of Ruth and not an original photo. My friend boasted of something but couldn't deliver the goods. It makes no sense to me when Christian leaders brag about their giftedness, skill level, and effectiveness in ministry and then can't deliver the goods. Instead, let's be aware of our anointing, walk confidently in it, and let the results speak for themselves. I would rather have people pleasantly surprised than disappointed about what I can give in my leadership to them. How about you?

CHALLENGE

What are your top strengths and gifts from God? How much do you talk about these gifts to others? Are you exaggerating them in any way? What can you do to let the results of your labor speak for themselves?

ACTION

_____

_____

_____

_____

_____

DAY 26: PROVERBS 26

VERSE

Do you see a person wise in their own eyes? There is
more hope for a fool than for them. (Proverbs 26:12)

THOUGHT

The word *fool* is mentioned ten times in the first eleven
verses of this Proverb. Each time, there is a stern warning against being a fool or interacting with a fool. The fool
doesn't seem to have much hope as it pertains to these
verses. However, the tables turn in verse 12, which says that
there is actually more hope for the fool than a person who
thinks they are wise in their own eyes. Ouch, what a lesson
in humility! The next time we think we have it all together
or all figured out, the next time we think we have it covered, the next time we think we have enough knowledge or
wisdom to face life on our own, we may just find ourselves
being looked down on by a fool.

CHALLENGE

In your own words, define God's grace. How does God empower you with His grace each day so you can rely on Him for your wisdom and provision? Identify any areas in which you are not freely receiving this grace and are trying to face life on your own. Ask God to pour out His grace upon you more today than ever before.

ACTION

DAY 27: PROVERBS 27

VERSE

One who is full loathes honey from the comb,
but to the hungry even what is bitter tastes sweet.
(Proverbs 27:7)

THOUGHT

For those who know me personally, they are aware of
my strong appetite for cookies, especially chocolate chip.
I could probably eat half a dozen, maybe more, with no
trouble at all given the opportunity. However, once I'm satisfied and have had enough, even my favorite cookie no
longer tastes good to me. The same thing happens when we
become satisfied and have had enough of the Lord. When
we say (maybe not verbally but with our lives), "I have what
I need. I'm full," the spiritual food He is feeding us causes
an upset soul. But when we hunger for more of the Lord
and keep a big appetite for His presence, anything and everything He gives us will be sweet to our soul. Even the
things we would rather not be fed taste good because we
are simply hungry for more.

CHALLENGE

Take the next several minutes right now and ask the Lord for more of Himself. Carry no agenda into this time; just begin crying out for more of the tangible glory of God in your life. Ask Him to reignite your appetite and hunger for His presence. At the end of this time, record anything He may have spoken or shown to you.

ACTION

_____

_____

_____

_____

_____

DAY 28: PROVERBS 28

VERSE

Whoever conceals their sins does not prosper, but the one who confesses and renounces them finds mercy. (Proverbs 28:13)

THOUGHT

As I was reading this verse, it struck me that both *confess* and *renounce* are included. When we confess our sins, we come into agreement with God that something in our lives does not match God's best for us. When we agree with Him, it puts His best for us into perspective, and it empowers us to fulfill His purposes. On the other hand, when we renounce our sin, we are refusing to recognize or abide by it and are formally declaring our abandonment of it. This is not just identifying that God has something better but also boldly declaring that we are no longer putting up with anything that is less than God's best for our lives.

CHALLENGE

Those who are following your leadership are depending on you to fulfill God's best for your life. Instead of spending time in self-introspection trying to come up with a list of all your sins, begin to jot down what you feel God has told you regarding His best for your life. If the Holy Spirit reveals anything you are currently involved with that is less than His best, come into agreement with Him by confessing it and break all ties by renouncing it. Then write a bold declaration stating your surrender to God and to only His best for your life!

ACTION

_____

_____

_____

_____

_____

DAY 29: PROVERBS 29

VERSE

If a ruler listens to lies, all his officials become wicked. (Proverbs 29:12)

THOUGHT

Your leadership has more influence in the lives of those around you than you can ever imagine. Think about the flow of leadership in this verse. A ruler listens to a lie, believes it, begins leading from the premises of that lie, and imparts it to his/her followers over a long period of time. As a result, the followers have received impartation and training based on a false foundation. If not corrected, these followers become wicked, literally meaning they become capable of doing harm to someone or something based on the way they were raised up. If taken in a positive light, just think about the kind of impact you will have when you listen to the truth of God's Word and the leading of the Holy Spirit. Consider the implications this will have on those who follow your example over a long period of time.

CHALLENGE

Think through several truths God has been revealing to you recently. How are you imparting those truths to those whom you influence? How are you guarding yourself from believing the lies that the enemy—and, many times, culture—throws at you?

ACTION

_____

_____

_____

_____

_____

DAY 30: PROVERBS 30

VERSE

Every word of God is flawless; he is a shield to those who take refuge in him. (Proverbs 30:5)

THOUGHT

I'm not sure there is anything flawless in the natural, something that is completely perfect, without any blemishes or shortcomings. But I do recognize the times I have seen something incredible, like the Changing of the Guard at the Tomb of the Unknown Soldier or a prestigious diamond ring that appears to be flawless through my own eyes. There is a seemingly uncontrollable force that holds my full attention and commands my respect for that moment. It creates a desire for me to get closer to these things, to observe more and to learn more. If we can look at things in the natural with this strong of an attraction, how much more should we approach every Word of God, which is completely and utterly flawless?

CHALLENGE

Is reading God's Word or listening to His voice frustrating, boring, or hard for you? Take time today to read Psalm 119 and draw close to David's heart and passion for God's Word. Allow God to remind you just how flawless and perfect His Word is.

ACTION

_____

_____

_____

_____

_____

DAY 31: PROVERBS 31

VERSE

A wife of noble character who can find? She is worth far more than rubies. (Proverbs 31:10)

THOUGHT

Instead of commenting on one verse or phrase, I saw verses 10–31 in a new light today. These verses are usually used in women's Bible studies about how women can be a wife of noble character. Instead, I propose using these verses in a men's study to paint the beautiful picture of what a Christian man should be looking for in a wife and how his leadership in her life can help develop these traits in her. Another element I noticed is how this "epilogue" brings all thirty-one Proverbs to a conclusion. It wasn't another warning about an adulterer. It wasn't a caution to avoid the fool. It was a clear target and vision that provided guidelines of something a young man could go after and give himself to. Though our leadership will require warnings and cautions, let us be remembered by the clear target and vision we have given to those we influence through our love, relationships, and ministry.

CHALLENGE

Take time to write an epilogue for a modern-day proverb you can teach to someone who looks up to you. Write a paragraph that explains a clear target or vision of what you see God doing in their life. Share it with them and begin to partner in prayer with them to see it come to fulfillment according to God's will.

ACTION

_____

_____

_____

_____

_____

CONCLUSION

My heart's desire is that you have experienced a positive change in your life through *Everyday Leadership*. Completion of this three-month study enables you to reflect on and act on ninety-three leadership principles from the book of Proverbs. If these principles are applied, they will have major practical and spiritual benefits in your life and in the lives around you. Just think about this for a minute: you have taken ninety-three moments in time to allow the Holy Spirit to give you supernatural revelation, in order that He may work through you in practical application. The outcome of how you lead more effectively today will have lasting results in generations to come.

Let me encourage you to now use *Everyday Leadership* as a written history of what God has revealed to you, a journal of what God has activated in you, and a guide for what God is able to do through you when facing the multitude of opportunities and challenges leadership brings.

I am so honored to be able to partner with you in leading more effectively. My dream on this side of eternity is to help equip and release people into their God-given destiny, and it humbles me to know that I have possibly assisted you in this area of following Jesus. Thank you for allowing me to join you on this part of your journey!

ABOUT THE AUTHOR

Kurt Jenkins is an ordained pastor in southwest Pennsylvania. He is married to his best friend, Charisse, and has four amazing children.

Kurt has always been an active member of the church body, providing him many life-changing opportunities. After several powerful encounters with God, Kurt sensed a definite transition in his life to leave his career as an elementary teacher and submit to the call of full-time ministry.

As a pastor, Kurt is passionate about helping to equip and release people into their God-given destiny and is motivated to see his community transformed in all areas through everyday leadership.